A souvenir guide

Seaton Delaval Hall

Northumberland

C000183393

National Trust

More than a Great House

Seaton Delaval Hall is a great house set in its own estate with lovely gardens and a fine collection; but it is also much more.

It is a signpost pointing to the diverse history of a family which acquired land here in the late 11th century. The house occupies the site of a Norman settlement, and its original Norman chapel remains in use today. The distinguished garden is the result of three centuries of development, and the surrounding park is still essentially intact. Both have significant surviving buildings and plantings, and both are vital in enhancing the house's scale, setting and dramatic impact.

Equally exceptional, but more unusual, are the vestiges of the industrial landscape, signs of the wider community's capacity for hard and dangerous work and its enterprising spirit; these fuelled the estate's development for

hundreds of years. In the 20th century Seaton Delaval Hall's fate remained entwined with that of the locality in which it sat. Damaged in the Great War, requisitioned for military use and for prisoners-of-war between 1939 and 1946, the house faced an uncertain future. As such, its revival after 1950 as a home, a focus for the estate, and a tourist attraction, is a vital part of its history.

The Hall

Built between 1719 and about 1730 for Admiral George Delaval, Seaton Delaval Hall is not only the finest house in the north-east, but also among the finest works of its architect, Sir John Vanbrugh, one of the masters of the

Above The north front of Seaton Delaval in the 1740s; painted by Arthur Pond

Opposite below John Delaval, the last of the direct Delaval line. He shared the family passion for dressing up; painted by William Bell in the 1770s

English Baroque. It is not as large as his earlier houses, Castle Howard and Blenheim Palace, but in its compact and integrated design, exquisite stonework, original detail and powerful sculptural presence it excels them.

Rising from the ashes

In 1822 the house was severely damaged by fire. Hundreds of local villagers rushed to help stem the flames, and total destruction was avoided. This disaster had a curious side-effect. The fire burnt out the central part of the house, but it also completely destroyed an added wing which had upset the symmetry of the design. The wing was not rebuilt; but the centre, after almost 40 years, was re-roofed to prevent further deterioration; even so, it has never been re-occupied. Although the west kitchen and servants' wing were remodelled to provide some accommodation, the house did not become a proper family residence again for more than a century after the fire.

It was successive owners who cared enough for the quality of the building to ensure its

survival. In particular Sir Jacob Astley, who was created 16th Lord Hastings in 1841, brought in John Dobson, the architect famed for Newcastle's Central Railway Station, to patch up and roof the central shell. Less than one hundred years later, the limitations of the first repair were recognised, and the late, 22nd Lord Hastings undertook from 1950 the major programme of stonework repairs and re-roofing which brought the house into the 21st century in a good condition.

Above A figure on the fireplace. A decorative detail in the Entrance Hall

A theatrical family

No less extraordinary are the characters of the Delaval family and the loyalty it inspired in the local community. From its beginnings, the estate has had a succession of owners with vision, energy, humanity and often humour.

The Delavals leap larger than life from the page. In Tudor times, old Sir John Delaval 'liberally spendeth his salt, wheat and mault like a gentleman'. Admiral George had the vision to employ Vanbrugh, but died after a fall from his horse and never saw his new home completed.

His nephew, Captain Francis Blake Delaval, finished the house and filled it with a family who became known as 'the Gay Delavals'. The captain's eldest son, handsome Sir Francis, was loved by all as an accidental military hero, practical joker and charmer of actresses; but as a stage-struck spendthrift he brought the estate to the brink of ruin.

The estate was rescued by his businesslike brother, Sir John Hussey Delaval, but the latter's only son John met an unfortunate early death.

There were various undutiful daughters, including the bewitching Lady Tyrconnel, renowned as 'the wildest of her race'. All were actors. No wonder the county flocked to their parties and plays. What a family indeed!

It's your Seaton Delaval

When Edward, the last of the Delavals, died in 1814, the property passed to his nephew Jacob, son of his sister, Rhoda, who had married Sir Edward Astley of Melton Constable in Norfolk. The Astleys' ancient title was revived in 1841 for their grandson, who became the 16th Lord Hastings. It was the deaths of the 22nd Lord Hastings and his wife in 2007 which brought their son, Delaval, 23rd Lord Hastings, to approach the National Trust. There followed a major fund-raising campaign, together with perhaps the largest consultation that the National Trust has ever conducted, inviting views as to whether the property should be

Above Martin Green and Valerie Fletcher – two of the local volunteers who are uncovering the history of Seaton Delaval Hall

Opposite Some of Seaton Delaval's devoted local supporters gathered in the Entrance Hall

Right One of the Queen Anne embroidered chairs in the Gallery

acquired, and, if it was, what it should be used for. The response was enormous; views were received from more than 100,000 people. The overwhelming response, that the National Trust should do its best to acquire the place, was backed with an amazing range of fund-raising ventures from major events to street collections; one young person even gave up using her mobile phone for a week and donated what she would have spent using it! The proceeds, backed with major grant-funding from both public and private sources, met the challenging target set by the National Trust, which had agreed to set aside from its own resources the largest amount it had ever allocated as an endowment.

Trying something different

No less important was the reaction that Seaton Delaval Hall, with its unusual character, should not be 'just another country house', but that its presentation and use should be the result of continuing consultation – adventurous, involving, changing, different. Above all, the place should continue to be, and should develop as, a focus for the local community with a very wide range of engaging and volunteering opportunities.

Much still to do

Through the efforts of many, and not least the generosity of Lord Hastings, the house, its gardens, a large portion of the estate, and the core of the collection, passed to the National Trust on 16 December 2009, and opened to visitors on May Day 2010. The speed of the change was deliberate. There was the tradition of opening in the summer months which stretches back to 1950. There was, too, a wish swiftly to acknowledge the help of all who had assisted with the acquisition, to show what was happening, and to give those who had volunteered a chance to get involved. And much remains to be done: services are outdated; visitor facilities are barely adequate; modifications are needed to allow for events and activities; conservation records must be compiled and collections catalogued.

We hope you will enjoy a place where there is still much progress being made, with the bustle which accompanies this, but where there are still secret and quiet places to enjoy.

Beginnings

The early Delavals

Among the men who scrambled ashore on that pebbly beach at Hastings in the late summer of 1066 was a group of knights from Laval in Normandy. They had come to support William, Duke of Normandy in his invasion of England and to gain land for themselves. It was William's son Rufus (William II) who eventually rewarded them for their assistance by granting them land in the old Saxon Earldom of Northumbria, when it was broken up around 1095. Hubert was the first named Delaval, his estate consisting of land at Black Callerton, Dissington, Seaton and Newsham. At Seaton Hubert found a small Saxon church, which he rebuilt and named the Church of Our Lady. He also built himself a small castle.

By the 13th century the stone tower at Seaton had become the main home of the Delavals. The family prospered, adding to their estates and taking a prominent part in administering the area. Sir John Delaval (d.1562) was five times sheriff of Northumberland. Other Delavals became border commissioners and played a part in trying to keep the peace on the county's northern frontier with Scotland. Sir Ralph Delaval (d.1628) was a border commissioner, JP and, with an income of over £1,000 per year, was one of the richest men in the county. He turned the old tower house into a Jacobean mansion. According to his son, 'He never affected drinking. Cards nor dice he never could abide them. He delighted much in the company of his kinsmen and friends and entertaining of strangers in his house.'

Sir Ralph's grandson (also called Ralph) showed deft footwork in moving from service in Richard Cromwell's parliament to being made a baronet by Charles II in recognition of his support at the Restoration and his work in creating Seaton Sluice (see p.8). In 1685 the second Sir Ralph moved out of the old Delaval mansion and into Seaton Lodge, a thatched house on the banks of Seaton Burn. Meanwhile, his son (yet another Ralph) married Diana, a daughter of Lord Delamere. The family was well off at this time and to ensure that any daughter of the union would make a good marriage, a clause was put into the marriage contract granting a dowry of

Below The Norman Church of Our Lady, c.1965

£8,000 on her union. By 1699 things were very different: Sir Ralph and his son were both dead, and the estate was in decline. Diana was a widow with a young daughter and, hoping to improve her situation, she married Sir Edward Blackett. Two months later, he married his son to Diana's daughter, who was just thirteen. Sir Edward then claimed the marriage dowry for his son, but the Delavals could not afford to pay it. When Diana died in 1713, Sir Edward again tried to claim the dowry, which, with interest, now amounted to over £14,000. Sir John Delaval, who held the Delaval estates, was unable to pay. Sir Edward then applied to the courts to seize the Delaval estates and bankrupt Sir John, who had no option but to sell up.

Two admirals in one family

Admiral Sir Ralph Delaval (1641-1707)

Admiral Sir Ralph Delaval was a member of the junior branch of the family, born at North Dissington, Ponteland. He began his naval career under the Duke of York (later James II), but survived James's fall to be knighted and promoted to the rank of Rear-Admiral of the Blue by William III. He suffered defeat off Beachy Head in 1690, but two years later was victorious over the French at the double battle of Barfleur-La Hogue. The following year, however, he was censured by Parliament for the loss of a convoy of merchantmen from Smyrna (now Ismir in Turkey), when 92 allied ships were sunk or captured. Stripped of his command, he retired to Northumberland. He never lived at Seaton Delaval, but is important to its story in the help he gave to his younger cousin George, who was also advancing in a naval career.

Admiral George Delaval (1668-1723)

Seaton Delaval was rescued by Admiral George Delaval of the Dissington branch of the family. As a younger son, George had inherited only £100 from his father, but he had made a

fortune from his naval and diplomatic careers, which brought him prize money and silver from the New World. He rose to national prominence as envoy to Moulay Ismail, the mercurial Sultan of Morocco, whose corsairs were emptying Christian ships and even coastal villages from the Mediterranean to the North Atlantic to provide slaves for the Sultan's building ventures. In 1700 Delaval traded a cargo of gunpowder and cannon for almost 200 English slaves. He also served as envoy to the king of Portugal from 1710 for three years; on his return he was elected as MP for West Looe, in Cornwall, and was eventually promoted Rear-Admiral.

By 1717 he was rich enough to be able to buy Sir John out of Seaton and Hartley, pay off Sir Edward Blackett and acquire the Shafto estate at Bavington. In 1718 he wrote to his brother, 'I would be glad to divert myself a little in my old age in repairing the old house, making a garden and planting forest trees.' In the event, he decided to go a great deal further.

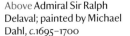

Above **Admiral Sir Ralph Delaval**; painted by Michael Dahl, c.1695–1700

Right **Admiral George Delaval**, builder of Seaton Delaval; painted by Sir Godfrey Kneller in 1710

Salt, coal and glass

The Seaton Delaval estate played an important part in Delaval family history, as it was responsible for a large proportion of the family's income for almost 700 years.

There had long been a coal and salt trade in and out of the existing natural harbour at the village of Hartley Pans (today's Seaton Sluice), but it was not until the late 17th century that it began to play a more important role in making the Delaval family fortune. Sir Ralph Delaval (1622–91) began the improvement process in 1690, when he made changes to the harbour by building sluice gates, which flushed the harbour silt out to sea, and a pier, allowing greater amounts of trade to pass through more easily. This was not a perfect solution, as collier brigs still had to load out at sea due to low water levels in the harbour.

During the 18th century the estate grew into one of the most important industrial estates in the north-east, with its primary industries being coal, salt and glass. The last, which became the Royal Northumberland Glassworks in the late 18th century, developed into one of the most successful industries on the estate, and indeed the largest bottle and jar producer in the whole country.

The transfer of control of the estates to Sir John Hussey Delaval in 1756 marks the real turning point in their history. He invested a large portion of the profits from the estate back into it in the form of improvements, expansion, housing for the workers, new technologies and ships. All of these resulted in an even greater return.

Left Seaton Sluice

Opposite top The Northumberland pitman

Opposite The Royal Northumberland Glassworks

Salt

The oldest industry on the estate was salt production, starting perhaps as early as the 14th century. Seawater was evaporated in huge pans heated over fires fuelled with coal mined on the estate. The salt produced was much sought after on the London market and still accounted for a significant amount of Sir John's fortune in the 18th century.

Coal

The largest and most profitable of the industries was coal. It was brought to the harbour from the coalfields to the south and west on wagonways and loaded into ships from boats just outside the harbour. High-quality Seaton Delaval coal was in great demand on the London market and sold at a premium.

Glass

Although the Royal Northumberland Glassworks were started from scratch in 1763, by 1777 production had reached 1,740,000 bottles a year. Its success was due largely to the ingenuity of John Delaval's younger brother, Tom, who had spent time studying glass and porcelain manufacture in Germany. Necessary raw materials were present on the estate to make the glass: coal, sand to be found in the harbour (possibly dumped ballast from the Thames estuary), and seaweed providing a plentiful supply of potash. Copperas or ferrous sulphate (a by-product of coal mining) coloured the glass, which was made into bottles and shipped down to London. The bottles were sent down to the harbour on narrow-gauge railways and loaded into 'bottle sloops' at the quayside. Like the coal, the established sea links and ports greatly increased sales.

The most important of John Delaval's improvements was the new entrance to the harbour made by cutting a channel 9.1m wide and over 16m deep through 243m of rock on the harbour's east side in 1764, and costing £10,000 (the equivalent of several millions today). Nicknamed the 'New Cut', it was designed to make it easier to load salt, coal and glass. The sluice gates at either end formed a deep-water dock where ships could be loaded afloat rather than out at sea. This meant that more colliers could make more journeys all year round rather than being weather-dependant. John, combining successful industrial activity with politics (as MP for Berwick), was eventually rewarded with a peerage becoming the first, and as fate decreed, also the last Lord Delaval.

Although agriculture brought in significant revenue from farm rents, the landscape around Seaton Sluice changed dramatically during the 18th century from a largely agricultural and rural one to a highly industrial one. Unfortunately, after Lord Delaval's death in 1808, his successors showed less direct interest in Seaton Delaval or the industries on its estate, and the fire of 1822 marked a turning point in its once industrially and economically rich history. Only the coal workings continued and then only on leases to others.

Seaton Delaval Hall

'The Admiral is very Gallant in his operation, not being dispos'd to starve the design at all, so that he is like to have a very fine Dwelling.'

Sir John Vanbrugh, 26 August 1721

The Tudor manor house

The earliest mention of a structure on the site is in 1415, when the tower of Seton de la Vale was held by Sir William Winchester. In 1549 the tower had a beacon basket for signalling with fire. A manor house was built onto the tower in Tudor times, with a hall, great chamber and various lodgings. Sometime before 1628 the house was extended with side-wings and long galleries; windows were inserted and chimneys and battlements added. By 1718 the buildings were in a state of decay.

Starting afresh

When Admiral George Delaval purchased the property in 1717, he was undecided as to whether he should restore the existing buildings or start afresh. By 1718 he had engaged Sir John Vanbrugh, who was given a free hand to design a small mansion for the Admiral's retirement. The result was the most remarkable structure of Vanbrugh's career. Stylistically, it is a reworking of the 'Castle Air' theme explored in his earlier country houses, but here, condensed to match his client's pocket, it proved much more effective.

In essence, Seaton Delaval is a gigantic 'play-house' in the Jacobean tradition, with reception rooms on the principal floor, bedrooms on the first floor, and a penthouse suite above for the Admiral. Set on its bastioned mount, it was a Baroque version of a Norman keep. Although the wings were not built exactly as shown in *Vitruvius Britannicus* (1721), they were essential to the design with their linking colonnades. Housing stables and kitchens, they were also essential to the running of the house.

As viewed from north and south, the overall silhouette of the central pile, with its attached corner and stair towers, is as forbidding as any of the region's medieval castles, while from every aspect its top storey looks like a huge Classical temple. To achieve this dramatic effect, Vanbrugh set the house on a large, raised rectangular platform, faced by a retaining wall with round corner-bastions and all protected by a boundary ditch. He then stacked up the relatively small amount of accommodation in the centre block to the height of four-and-a-half storeys.

Storytelling in stone

Vanbrugh incorporated in the north front architectural features which indirectly reflected his patron's rank and calling. Hence the 'strong' militaristic Doric columns flanking the entrance, the 'porthole' windows to the attic space of the belvedere, and its surrounding roof terrace laid out like the quarterdeck of one of the Admiral's men-of-war.

More obvious references carved in the stonework include Roman military insignia, naval guns, an admiral's cockaded hat, harpoons, Neptune's trident and sea creatures, with a central Delaval coat-of-arms

Above Sir John Vanbrugh, architect of Seaton Delaval; painted by Sir Godfrey Kneller c.1704–10

within the gable pediment. If anyone doubts Vanbrugh's genius as one of England's foremost architects, they will surely be convinced by what he achieved on this wind-swept site, where, had he lived, the Admiral would have been able to 'review' passing ships from the windows of his belvedere 'look-out'. As it was, both architect and patron would be dead before the house was completed.

Finishing the house

When the Admiral died in 1723, aged 62, after falling from his horse, the hall was still over five years from completion. Although he was a wealthy man, one wonders if he had realised quite what he had undertaken. When his nephew, Capt. Francis Blake Delaval, succeeded to the property in 1723, the impracticality of the design for normal living became obvious. Although not all families need bedrooms for a dozen children, the arrangement of the ground-floor rooms allowed the winds to blow through them unobstructed from north to south. There is some doubt as to when (or even whether)

wings were added both east and west of the main block, but they appear on a series of paintings and engravings from 1745 onwards. The lower parts of these wings seem to have followed soon after the completion of the main block. This could also explain the extended building period. Perhaps enough of the main block had been completed before the alterations to enable Vanbrugh to see his creation standing proudly above the coast, before his death in 1726. The work was probably supervised by William Etty, Vanbrugh's clerk of works at Castle Howard.

The Captain's sons, Sir Francis and Sir John (later Lord Delaval), each made additions to allow for entertaining and the latter's growing family. Of these changes the most noticeable was the addition in about 1771 of an extra storey to the south wings, which appear in William Bell's paintings of 1775.

Above **The garden front**

Below left **The cornice is decorated with military symbols that celebrate Admiral Delaval's naval exploits**

Below **The entrance front**

The gay Delavals

Below left Captain Francis Blake Delaval c.1730

Below right Rhoda Apreece, painted by John Vanderbank in 1725, the year after her marriage to Captain Blake Delaval

Opposite The new stables were the setting for a surprise banquet in the 1760s

Captain Francis Blake Delaval and his wife Rhoda moved into the newly built house in 1728 and over the next twenty years had twelve children. It was during this period that the Delavals gained their reputation for fun-loving and outrageous behaviour, which probably increased as the children grew up. Captain Francis was busy running the estate, while his wife, exhausted from child-bearing, let her growing brood slip out of her grasp. These wild, undisciplined children, under the leadership of the eldest boy, Francis, encouraged travelling players and entertainers to call at the hall and instigated the practical jokes for which the Delavals became notorious.

Rhoda Apriece Wife of Fran: Blake Delaval Esq:

A perfect fairy land

A visitor described Delaval Hall as like an 'Italian Palace and the grounds were a perfect fairy land of light, beauty and music'. It was theatrical entertainment that the Delavals liked best, and they started producing and performing in plays themselves. The whole family took part, and everyone in the neighbourhood was invited to watch. With liberal amounts of beer and wine flowing, a riotous evening was had by all. Francis invited the local estate workers to puppet shows, ass-racing, grinning matches, sack races and, it is said, even competitions to bite the heads off sparrows!

Bedroom pranks

Going to bed could be an unnerving experience at Delaval Hall. Guests would retire to their bedrooms, and while they were undressing, mechanical hoists would suddenly raise the bedroom walls, exposing them to public view. In one bedroom there was a four-poster bed which could be lowered into a tank of cold water, complete with occupants, by winding a handle in the room next door. In another room drunken guests would be put to bed in the dark, and awaken in the morning to find themselves lying on the ceiling. The room was completely inverted, the chairs and tables were stuck to the ceiling, and the chandelier was in the middle of the floor.

Shortly after the stables were remodelled with stone stalls around 1765, Francis invited the local gentry to a banquet. When the guests arrived, they found the place deserted and in darkness. Confused and irritated, they were just about to leave, when the doors to the new stables were thrown open to reveal a superb feast set out around the new stalls.

Sir Francis Blake Delaval

Above Lord Delaval's headstrong daughter Sarah; by Richard Cosway, 1780s

The most notorious of the Delavals was Sir Francis Blake Delaval, the eldest son of Captain Blake Delaval. The serious things in life did not interest Sir Francis: he sold his inheritance for an annuity to his younger brother John, whom he left to manage the family estates. He was well known for playing practical jokes, but his first love was the theatre.

When Francis was about twenty, his cousin Susanna and a young friend of hers, Betty Roach, came to Delaval Hall. John eventually married Susanna, but Frances seduced the poor unfortunate Betty, who became his mistress and had two illegitimate children by him. Tiring of Seaton, Francis moved to London, where he fell in with a group of dissolute actors led by Samuel Foote. Francis fitted nicely into this world. He was at ease with everyone and soon became friends with Prince Edward, the younger brother of George III.

An accidental hero

Possibly to avoid his debtors, he became at one stage a soldier and took part in a raid on the French coast. Tipped from the first boat to reach the shore into cold water, he led the charge up the beach and took part in the 'glorious' burning of St Malo. Returning as a hero to England, he was honoured with a Knighthood of the Bath by the new king George III. The lack of any serious opposition to the raid was tactfully overlooked.

A life of pleasure

Francis enjoyed mainly the life of an idle gentleman, but could not afford it, as he was always in debt. Foote decided that the solution was to find Francis a rich wife. His candidate was Isabella, Lady Paulet, an elderly widow with a fortune of £100,000, who was looking for a husband. To persuade Lady Isabella to marry Francis, Foote dreamt up an elaborate charade, using a bogus fortune teller and a prearranged accidental meeting. The ruse worked, and in March 1750 they were married. The following year Francis spent

A SRATH SPEY
In a few Days wil

Opposite Sir Francis Blake Delaval, the spendthrift eldest son of Captain Delaval; after Reynolds

Right John Hussey, Lord Delaval, who rescued the estate from his wayward brother, Sir Francis, painted by William Bell, 1770s

Below *A Strath spey or new Highland reel as danced at Seaton Delaval*. Lord Delaval's daughter Sarah had several lovers, including the Duke of York (hiding under the bed) and Lord Strathmore (on the left); published 1790

£1,500 on hiring the Drury Lane Theatre in London to stage *Othello*, with the family taking all the leading parts. The House of Commons adjourned two hours early so that MPs could attend the performance. Unfortunately for Francis, however, Lady Isabella's fortune was only £24,000, which was soon spent.

Francis continued to live with Betty rather than his wife, who sued him for adultery, but lost the case. Isabella faded out of Francis's life and died in obscurity. In 1763 Francis saw a young Ann Catley playing the nymph Sabrina. He was captivated by her, and soon they were living together. When her father heard where she was living, he sued Francis for debauching his daughter. The court found Francis guilty and awarded costs against him. At the end of the proceedings, a very pregnant Ann left the court arm-in-arm with Francis.

Francis spent his time and money socialising and gambling. He introduced his recently divorced sister Anne to Prince Edward, who began an affair with her. In 1767 the Prince died suddenly. Francis was deeply affected by his friend's death, took to drink, and became grossly overweight. In August 1771, after a huge meal he collapsed and died, alone except for his servant. He left at least five illegitimate children and a pile of unpaid debts. Was his a wasted life? Perhaps, but popular tradition associates him with fashionable amusement and gay revelry. He had a huge funeral and was mourned by many.

Triumph and disaster:
The 19th century

The Astley inheritance

Edward Delaval, the last legitimate male member of the family, died in 1814, bequeathing Seaton Delaval Hall to his nephew, Sir Jacob Henry Astley, who already owned a large 17th-century country house in Norfolk, Melton Constable. Having employed the Newcastle architect John Dobson to make designs for remodelling Seaton Delaval, Sir Jacob died in 1817. His son, also Sir Jacob (but re-created 16th Lord Hastings in 1841), seems to have done little more at this stage. The house was left in the care of Mr Huthwaite, a longstanding house servant. Then came disaster.

The fire

At dusk on 3 January 1822 sailors off Whitley Bay noticed that the sunset seemed unusually brilliant. Seaton Delaval Hall was on fire. The *Newcastle Chronicle* reported the disaster:

> Every endeavour to preserve the body of the building was unavailing nothing but the bare walls being left standing. The fire is generally supposed to have originated in a chimney which had been rendered foul by birds having built their nests in it, and that hence the fire was communicated to a rafter fixed to the chimney. The roof was speedily in flames and the fire burnt with such fury as to bid defiance to all human efforts. The glass in the windows … was reduced to a liquid state and the lead in the roof poured down like water.

Although Vanbrugh's central block was completely gutted, the local people who rushed to the scene managed to save the kitchen and stables wings, together with family portraits, furniture and archives. The centre remained a roofless ruin until about 1859–60, when the now very senior John Dobson was again called upon by the 16th Lord Hastings to produce a comprehensive restoration scheme. Walltops were rebuilt to support a new roof, and cast-iron columns were used to strengthen internal walls. But the scheme faltered, and the place was left an unheated and unfurnished shell. Dobson himself was candid about the practical drawbacks of Vanbrugh's creation:

> Sir John's general plan was to enter the building direct from the north into a magnificent hall, with corridors leading right and left; the consequence was that the current of air from the exterior was unchecked, and rendered the building in cold weather almost uninhabitable. Lord Strathmore … complained to me of the want of comfort in the house, and that he felt obliged always to have an extra cloak with him when residing there.

The 1862 Hartley pit disaster

After Lord Delaval's time mines were leased to independent companies. Pits in the area had always been vulnerable to flooding from sea water, which had to be pumped out with powerful beam engines. On 16 January 1862, the iron beam of the pumping engine above the New Hartley Colliery suddenly snapped, blocking the mine shaft with hundreds of tons of masonry and timber and trapping 204 men and boys underground A rescue team worked without a break for seven days and nights, but found that all had suffocated. The Hartley pit disaster was one of the worst tragedies in British mining history, but it led to improved standards and the principle of every pit having two shafts. However, it effectively spelt the end of coal mining at Seaton Sluice. Other industry was also in decline. The bottle works closed in 1870, and the sea gradually washed away the wharves. All that is left today is the New Cut.

Above The night after the pit disaster

Left The 16th Lord Hastings, who rescued Seaton Delaval after the fire

Right *Melton with Fred Archer up*. In 1885 Melton won the coveted 'double' of the Derby and the St Leger

Below The Forecourt in 1817; watercolour by John Dobson

Won by a head

From their Norfolk home, Melton Constable, the Lords Hastings took a serious interest in horse racing. George, 20th Lord Hastings won the 1885 Derby with his colt, Melton, ridden by the greatest jockey of the age, Fred Archer. *The Times* recorded the final stages of the race: 'Further and further did Paradox draw away, and his victory seemed well assured until Melton coming with a run, drew into second place. Inch by inch Melton crept up, and despite Archer's most strenuous endeavours, the bell was reached ere Lord Hastings's colt could get on terms. In the short run home from this point a truly magnificent race resulted, and as Melton and Paradox answered gamely to every call that was made upon them the finish was so close that until Melton's number was hoisted no one could say with certainty which was the winner.'

Late Victorian Seaton Delaval

While the family never abandoned Seaton Delaval Hall, its condition allowed only fleeting occupation. Even so, part of the garden was maintained, and the grounds became a focus for community activities. In 1891 Lord Hastings gave the private Chapel of Our Lady to be the church for the new parish of Seaton Delaval. By 1900 there were garden parties and church fêtes, cricket was played on the south lawn, and the Mahogany Room was used for meetings. In the courtyard, artillery displays foreshadowed a more military role for the Hall.

Seaton Delaval in two wars

A poet at Seaton Delaval

The war poet and composer Ivor Gurney of the Gloucestershire Regiment retrained as a signalman after he had been gassed at the third battle of Ypres in 1917. He was based at Seaton Delaval from November 1917 until July 1918, but spent some time in hospital between February and June suffering from stomach problems and depression. Letters to his friends reveal that he was not happy at camp, as nobody was interested in poetry and he was not motivated to write much. He reported that he did signalling operation three nights a week. He called it 'a freezing, ugly, uncomfortable Hell of a Hole'.

In the patriotic fervour that greeted the outbreak of the First World War in 1914, hundreds of local men joined the Territorial Army or the Volunteer Battalions. 'D' Company of the 3rd Battalion, the Northumberland Volunteers was based at Seaton Delaval, where they trained in the evenings and at weekends. A camp was set up in the Vicarage Field to house the Tyne Garrison, which was responsible for coastal defence. After the war the camp buildings were taken over by Dr Barnardo's, who brought children in their care for holidays here: 'Many amongst them had never before known the joys of a summer holiday in the open air, and it was good to see their ruddy happy faces while at their exercises and play.'

A prisoner-of-war camp in the Second World War

After victory at El Alamein in 1943 and the subsequent invasion of Italy, thousands of German prisoners of war were brought to England. Many of those taken to the north-east to work on the land were interned at Seaton Delaval Hall for the rest of the war. Their presence in Seaton Sluice had a lasting effect on the lives of many local residents, and the prisoners never forgot the fair treatment they received. You can still see notices in German in the house.

The prisoners rose at 5am and paraded in the courtyard by 6. Most were taken by bus or lorry to work on local farms, threshing wheat, picking potatoes or digging drains. Food was

Left The poet and composer Ivor Gurney was stationed at Seaton Delaval during the First World War

Below You can still see notices written in German for the benefit of the Second World War POWs

uppermost in the minds of many POWs – hardly surprising when one considers the meagre rations they received for an eight-hour day of heavy manual labour:

Breakfast: 1 piece of cake, 1 slice of bread with margarine and marmalade, 1 cup of tea with milk and sugar.
Dinner: Beef goulash, mashed dried peas, boiled potatoes.
Supper: 1/3 of loaf of bread, 100 grams of marmalade, 50 grams of margarine, cocoa with milk.

At Christmas the POWs turned their skills to making wooden toys to sell, including hen-peckers and heart-shaped love-token boxes. They consumed so much wood that very few window sills survived the war.

Right The POWs whiled away the time making wooden toys

An artist at Seaton Delaval

In 1941 the painter John Piper, who had been recording bomb-damaged buildings, visited Seaton Delaval:

There on the right is the great forecourt that now grows grass for hay. The central block faces down the slight slope of the court, the colonnaded wings embrace it on two other sides. Ochre and flame-licked red, pock-marked and stained in purplish umber and black, the colour is extremely up-to-date: very much of our times. And not the colour only. House and landscape are seared by the east wind that blows from Germany, and riven with fretting industrialism, but they still withstand the noise and neglect, the fires and hauntings of twentieth-century life. Its main block an untenanted stone shell, the Hall is somehow alive, unlike many stately homes.

Piper loved the untamed quality of the place, hoping, when the war was over, for 'permanent bank holiday crowds, with much shouting, steam organs, and plenty of fireworks at night'.

Exploring Seaton Delaval Hall

'Something of the castle air.'
Sir John Vanbrugh

The Approach

In Seaton Delaval Hall's heyday, most visitors would have arrived by carriage from the Great North Road to the west. Passing between great pillars, they would have had an increasing sense of anticipation as they progressed along well over a mile of the great western avenue with double files of lime trees on each side. The drive swung to the north, opening a prospect of the sea and, suddenly, the house appeared on the right. The effect was meant to be, and is still, breathtaking.

The Forecourt

The house was always approached from the main road to the north across a sunk fence, or ha-ha. The present gate screen was designed and supervised 50 years ago by Frederick Hetherington, resident agent. The centre of the house and the wings are part of a single design and all are vital to the working of the whole. The wings embrace the space and provide actual shelter with arcades; but the centre has no projecting portico; its six columns are grouped as if pushed aside like curtains on rails around the corners of the central bay, so that the end columns disappear behind the others. This makes the angled views of the main block particularly monumental.

Sculpture

David and Goliath
In the middle of the forecourt stands an 18th-century lead copy, possibly by John Cheere, of an unidentified 16th-century Italian marble, apparently lost, by either Baccio Bandinelli or a follower of Giambologna.

Above **The East Wing, which contains the stables**

Below **The massive columns are grouped at the corners of the central bay**

It once stood on one of the corner bastions of the garden. Having been stolen and cut in pieces in the 1980s, the remains were retrieved and repaired and set up in this position for greater security.

The East Wing

It contains stables, harness rooms and carriage houses. In its triangular pediment over the centre was a wind indicator – useful for gauging the arrival and departure of sailing ships from the harbour at Seaton Sluice. (For interior, see p.30.)

The West Wing

The West Wing housed the domestic services, with the Great Kitchen in the middle and rooms to each side for stores, laundry and other servants' rooms. In 1752 a fire damaged the Kitchen, but, with much help from local residents, it was prevented from doing serious harm to the central block. (For interior, see p.32.)

The Central Block

It was not just the middle of the house, but also the heart of the estate. Here the family lived with space for entertaining, with service quarters in the raised basement and servants' bedrooms under the roof. It was also the centre of the design, the most elaborate and impressive part of the house where Vanbrugh let off his most spectacular architectural fireworks. Mounting the steps to the front door, you become aware of the vigorous stone carving, the great columns with their horizontal rustication, the variety of classical carvings with symbols appropriate to a sailor and a naval officer, the deep cornices and, above all, in the triangular pediment, the Delaval family arms set in an array of nautical and military weaponry.

Right *David and Goliath*; an 18th-century copy of a 16th-century Italian statue in the Forecourt

The Entrance Hall

The Entrance Hall was designed to impress visitors with its monumental scale and quality. Its walls, two full storeys high, are all of finely carved stone with arcading at both levels (and originally with a vaulted plastered ceiling); sculpture was concentrated around the chimneypiece and in the upper arcades where figures represent the arts – architecture, painting, music and sculpture – and geography and astronomy – the earthly and heavenly spheres. Although repaired, much of the black and white marble floor is original. As with many of Vanbrugh's houses, a balcony at the inner end provides access between staircases and bedrooms. It is supported on massive corbels, or carved brackets, which contrast with the delicate decorative ironwork that supports the handrail.

The Mahogany Parlour

This is one of two rooms in the Central Block which survived the fire of 1822. Its panelling was put up in 1726, when the clerk of works reported that two men were 'sett on to wainscot the North Easte Roome with Mahoggony wood, which is so well dryed that it works extremely fine'. With dark panels reaching above the dado, or chair rail, the full height of the walls up to a vigorously carved frieze, the room still gives some idea of the original character of the house's reception rooms. Much damaged, the room was repaired by the late Lord Hastings and opened to visitors in 1962.

Pictures

Family portraits include the present Lord Hastings's grandparents on the south wall, and great-grandparents on the west (fireplace) wall; and, as a child, Sir Jacob Henry Astley, who owned Seaton Delaval Hall between 1859 and 1871, and saved the fire-damaged central block by re-roofing it c.1860.

The Mahogany Parlour Closet

This corner turret room also retains much of its original panelling. The double doors each move only 45 degrees and, when closed, form part of the panelling of the Mahogany Parlour, disguising the entrance; this must have been a quiet place set apart from the hubbub of the main house.

The East Stair

The oval staircase is an engineering wonder, with each step a single stone fitted to its neighbours without central support. The ironwork handrail melted by the fire has been left at the upper levels; the lower part was reconstructed by Messrs M. Aynsley & Sons Ltd of Newcastle in 1961–2. The staircase leads up to the upper floors or down to the basement.

The Passage to the East Stair

It still has a smoke-blackened ceiling. Just before the stairs, on the left, a narrow angled passage was cut through the original stonework to give access to a corridor in the added East Wing. The fire of 1822 is thought to have started in this wing, destroying it and gutting the central block.

Opposite far left **The Entrance Hall**

Left **The East Stair**

Below **The ironwork handrail on the spiral staircase was melted in the fire**

The Basement

It is not a fully sunken cellar, but an important part of the house's design. It reaches well above ground level, allowing windows to give good light, and also raises the *piano nobile*, or principal floor, to give it greater prominence.

The basement has castle strength with all the chambers having vaulted ceilings. Here is some of the most skilful stonework in the house. It seems to have been the strength of the basement which prevented the whole house collapsing at the time of the fire. Although this was an area largely used by servants, the separation of family and guests from servants in the early 18th century was far less rigorous than it later became. It is not hard to imagine guests being taken down to admire the central corridor with its sculpture niches and finely groined vaults. Originally all the floors were flagged with stone. There are four main chambers in the corners each with a good fireplace and an extension into the base of its corner turret. A surviving plan shows their late Georgian (and possibly original) uses: **Housekeeper's Room** (NE); **Servants' Hall** (NW) and **Footmen's Room** (SW).

The Steward's Room (SE) has a corner strong room with the date '1753' pierced into its iron door. In the middle, running out under the porticos, were **beer cellars** (south) and **wine cellars**, **pantry** and **scullery** (north).

Above One of the vaulted service rooms in the abandoned basement

Opposite The Gallery offers a good view of the statues in the niches in the upper level of the Entrance Hall

The Seaton Delaval servants in January 1800

Steward's Room

Ann Farley	Ladies Maid
Mr Bryan	Music Master
Mrs Bryers	

Servants' Hall

Edward and John Morgan	Footmen
William Ages and A. Hadlow	1st and 2nd Coachmen
William Smithers and Boy	Grooms
John Dobson and Ray Smith	Gamekeepers
An additional helper	
Ann Dodsworth	House Maid
Elizabeth Cook	Assistant House Maid
Sarah Vaughan	Cook
Elizabeth Woodcock	Scullery Maid

The West Stair

It is like its twin to the east but seems to have had more rebuilding. The doorway (blocked) just above basement level was the original access to the Kitchen Wing passage. It leads up to the principal floor and up again to the Gallery corridor, which originally led to the main bedrooms and, above these, to the attics.

From the Gallery you get a closer view of the Entrance Hall sculpture and can see how the figures were built with textile and plaster around armatures; real textile was pinned to the figures and plastered to look like textile! Originally, there were no views to the south, only a corridor to bedrooms.

The Tapestry Room
The Gilt Parlour
The Saloon

The Tapestry Room

It retains some original woodwork. Restoration in 1962 included wallpaper put up in imitation of earlier fabric wall coverings.

Pictures

Two views of Seaton Delaval Hall, of 1775 by William Bell.
Charles I, a studio version of Van Dyck's celebrated portrait in the Louvre.
Isabella, Regent of the Netherlands, after (and indeed far from) Rubens.

The Gilt Parlour

To the west of the Entrance Hall, it is one of only four rooms on the principal floor. Its historic name suggests that it might have been a light room with gilt decoration that glittered in the evening sun. Unlike the Mahogany Parlour, it lost all its ceiling, panelling and other fittings either in the fire or during the following period, when the house was left roofless for almost 40 years.

It is sometimes called the Mantrap Room because of the three mantraps displayed on its chimney wall. Designed to discourage poaching and other unwanted activities on estate grounds, especially at night, the traps were strong enough when triggered by stepping on the plate to break legs between the closing 'jaws'. These traps were brought, as rather grim decorations, from the family's Norfolk estates about 60 years ago.

The Saloon

The Saloon was the main gathering, meeting and entertaining room in the 18th-century house. Here the Delavals held their celebrated parties and amateur theatricals – with music and laughter and riotous behaviour.

This great single room (23m long and 9m wide) was divided into three parts with pairs of columns; the stone capitals of the original eight columns stand on the floor. Originally decorative plaster ceilings by 'Vercelli' (probably Francesco Vassalli, an itinerant Italian *stuccatore* who worked at Castle Howard) framed three ceiling pictures. The room was warmed by two fireplaces in the north wall; that to the east has a much later insertion, possibly from the time when the

Opposite **The Saloon**

Below **Mantraps in the Gilt Parlour**

room was used by soldiers or even prisoners-of-war. Small turret rooms in the outer corners provided some privacy and quiet away from the bustle of the main space.

This part of the house suffered the worst damage during the fire of 1822. The cast-iron columns were part of the repairs carried out by John Dobson c.1860, when much of the upper walls had to be rebuilt. The iron columns, not unlike those used by Dobson about this time at Newcastle railway station, were intentionally very thin so that, while they were strong enough to support the walls above, they could be hidden within artificial marble (scagliola) columns the size of the originals. The repair project remained incomplete; the resulting roofed shell, showing original fabric with repaired sections, is interesting in its own right, and reveals the arrangement of rooms on the upper levels.

The Gardens

Opposite above Lady Hastings, who revived the garden; painted by Vasco Lazzolo in 1966

Opposite below *Samson slaying the Philistine* in the Rose Garden

Below The Rose Garden

Access to the gardens is by the South Portico, which is supported on six giant fluted Ionic columns. On sunny afternoons this must have been a favourite place to sit with optional shade and views over the invisible ha-ha to the Obelisk (1741) exactly half a mile away in the middle of the great informal landscape. Even more distant in a gap in woods to the left of the Obelisk are ruins of Tynemouth Priory, which the Delavals supported at least as far back as 1135.

The portico survived the fire, but was in such poor condition that it had to be rebuilt with a new frieze in 1960–2. Original stonework removed at that time is arranged nearby on the South Lawn.

The South Lawn

This small paddock was used as a cricket field between the wars, and is now a play area. Originally, it was lined with formal trees that framed the south vista, which continued beyond the ha-ha with views to the distant Obelisk. This formal landscape was gradually made more 'natural' in tune with the changing fashions of the 18th century.

The West Lawn

The weeping ash is said to have been planted in the mid-18th century. The semi-circular border is a hundred years younger, but its present planting owes a great deal to the late Lady Hastings. The little sundial came from Melton Constable.

To the south Lady Hastings replanted a dense shrubbery with select rhododendrons and azaleas and opened up views to the church.

The Parish Church (former Private Chapel) of Our Lady

Beyond the paling with gate is the former private chapel, which became the parish church in 1891, and is often opened by its own volunteers. It has changed little since it was consecrated in 1102 and is the only obvious witness to the vanished medieval settlement with its tower and later manor house.

The Rose Garden

This was established in the 19th century to the south of the kitchen wing with box hedges framing beds of roses. At its west end is a statuary group of *Samson slaying the Philistine*, a copy in lead, possibly by John Cheere, of the original marble by Giambologna, which is now in the Victoria & Albert Museum in London.

The Formal Garden

The North-west Parterre or Formal Garden of 1950 was one of the earliest designs of James Russell of Sunningdale Nurseries, who later achieved international recognition as a garden designer. It has been meticulously maintained over the past 25 years by the head gardener, Terry Hewison. The fountain, centrepiece to the lower level, and the urns were later embellishments. The lead cistern on the east terrace and the distinguished 18th-century iron gates, bearing Constable and Astley arms, at the west yard both came from Melton Constable.

Sculpture

A lead figure of *Diana the huntress* stands on the north-west bastion, one of the four corner bastions of the original garden enclosure. From here the size of the enclosing ha-ha walls, nine feet high, can be appreciated, with views over the Formal Garden to the house. The seated stone statue at the gate to the Privy Garden may be a shepherdess. Her flock, scattered about the garden, is being gathered – and a fold will be found.

The Privy Garden

This was created inside yew hedges from a cabbage patch by Lady Hastings with a pond, a summer-house, and, as a surprise, a Laburnum tunnel with a statue of the French *Crown Prince Imperial* by Joseph Bosio of 1829.

The East Wing and beyond

The East Wing was built at the same time as the main block and completed early in the 1730s. A rainwater head, now used as a lamp shade over the entrance door, bears the date 1732, although this seems to have come from the main block. The main variation from Vanbrugh's original design was the curved projection of the east wall, which provided a useful covered space for working on the horses.

The Stables

The interior was refitted with stone stalls c.1765 after Sir Francis Blake Delaval had been impressed by the stables at Hopetoun House. Although the stalls appear at first sight to be all stone built, the kicking posts at the ends are of timber treated to look like stone. The names above the stall are those of the horses who lived here around 1800 in Lord Delaval's time. A large bran bin and a saddle rack await the horses' return. The smaller stable at the south end of the range later became an estate office, and now serves as a small tea shop. The pavilion at the north end of the wing once served as a harness room and later as the office of the resident agent. Its companion at the north end of the west wing has been a ticket office and small shop for 60 years.

To the east of the Stables are the Ice-house, buried in its earth mound, and the Old Brewhouse with its vaguely triumphal brick façade; it was later used as estate workshops and to house a collection of carriages and other estate vehicles.

Still further east in the **Walled Garden** with the temporary car-park (2010) are the **Orangery** (c.1735), a central pool once ornamented with sculpture, and an old doorway in the south wall, which looks 17th-century and may have belonged to the old manor house.

Opposite The view from the portico towards the Obelisk

Below The stalls in the Stables were built from stone

The Landscape

The wider historical estate is protected as a Conservation Area. It is equally important in providing a grand setting for the hall. The remains of ornamental planting – shelter belts, screens, park margins – follow a pattern well established by the early 19th century (and probably much earlier, had the evidence survived). They assist the inner plantings to frame or emphasise viewpoints, and to screen that which was not regarded as scenic.

Here, too, are buildings and water features: the ill-fated Mausoleum, which was never consecrated due to a feud with the Bishop of Durham; Starlight Castle, built as a vantage-point from which to admire the southern part of the park and the coast; and, most prominent of all, the great Obelisk, on the projection of the main axis of the house. The interestingly shaped Egg Pond is situated exactly between the two. Now set in arable land, it would once have been a more formal feature, providing serene reflections for strollers or, according to one account, a bathing place.

The estate had two dramatic extensions,

both of which remain substantially intact. To the west is a great tree-lined avenue (see p.20). To the east, the Sea Walk gave discrete access from the Hall, through the walled gardens, to the shipping and associated industrial activity of the busy harbour at Seaton Sluice. This may be a very old route, because it appears to be the most direct way to get from the manorial site to the coast.

The significance of the estate does not stop at the limits of the ornamental planting and historic parkland. Seaton Delaval always had wider geographical and social horizons. The house was always designed to make the most of distant views: northward towards the Cheviot Hills, and southward to the coast and the ruins of Tynemouth Priory (long supported by the Delavals through the payment of tithes). Today, this classic north-east panorama is enlivened with layers of residential development on the horizon, and perhaps most poignantly, considering the area's coal-powered heritage, the blades of giant wind turbines at Blyth harbour.

The West Wing

The Main Entrance Lobby

It was created by enclosing a section of the west arcade c.1960 to act as a lobby to the Old Kitchen, when it started to be used for entertaining.

Sculpture

North window sill: two white marble busts of boys: *Albert Edward Delaval Astley, 21st Lord Hastings* (1882–1956) and his brother *Captain Welton Astley*, by G.E. Wade, 1891.
South window sill: *Crouching Venus*, early 19th-century French bronze based on Roman original.

Furniture

Carved walnut box *settle*, Normandy, 19th-century, but with panel from a 16th-century chest; with scrolled cresting and central mask of a 'green man'.

The Old Kitchen

Once this was a hive of cooking activity, where meals were produced for the whole household; its two-storey height allowed for smoke and steam and heat. The space has unusually sophisticated architecture for a kitchen with general symmetry, arched recesses and pilasters supporting the soaring roof vaults. Here, too, are the only pointed arches in the house. The westward-curved projection with its wide three-part Palladian window enhances both the space and the light.

Another curiosity is the window in the east wall, which gave a little light, but also allowed those on the gallery to see what was happening in the kitchen.

Pictures

East wall

Right arched recess: *Admiral George Delaval*, by Sir Godfrey Kneller, 1710.
Left arched recess: *Captain Francis Blake Delaval, RN*, c.1730.
Upper wall: *Two views of Seaton Delaval Hall*, by Arthur Pond, 1743.
Above doorway: *Small view of the north front of Seaton Delaval Hall*, c.1750.

North wall

Above boilers: *The Delaval family*: Rhoda

Above **The Old Kitchen**

Left *Sir Jacob Astley*; copy by Rhoda Delaval of the 17th-century original

Opposite *The Gay Delavals*; from the circle of Joseph Highmore, c.1744–5

Delaval, eldest child of Captain Francis Blake Delaval, with three brothers, Francis, John and Edward, and three sisters. There were five other brothers; altogether, they were the 'Gay Delavals'; painted c.1744-5 under the influence of Joseph Highmore.

South wall

Above fireplace: *Sir Jacob Astley, 3rd Bt, and his family*, including Edward, the small boy in grey with a dog, who was to marry Rhoda Delaval. Their son, Jacob Henry, eventually inherited Seaton Delaval. Painting attributed to Petrus van Reyshoot.

West wall

Portraits of the Astley family, including a copy by Rhoda Delaval of the portrait of Sir Jacob Astley, the Royalist infantry general. The original, once believed to be by Van Dyck, hangs over the right doorway on the south wall.

Armour

Two suits of 'head-to-foot' fluted *armour*, made in south Germany around 1530.
A steel target *shield*, etched and gilt; south German, probably from Nuremberg, about 1560.

Furniture

Includes: *cabinet on stand* with fine ebony and ivory internal decoration, Antwerp, c.1560; two sets of six *walnut chairs*, 1680s, from the latter years of Charles II; pair of walnut *desk chairs* with early woven 'carpet' seat covers, c.1730, George II; circular *hall table* with frieze drawers (sometimes called a rent table, at which tenants made payments), late 18th-century, possibly Irish; longcase regulator *clock*, c.1820, dial signed by G. Rossi, Norwich.

Modern sculpture

Includes: bronze head of the late Lord Hastings; two stone sculptures, a brown kneeling figure and a green bust; Zimbabwe (where Lord Hastings had a farm), c.1980.

The North Passage (or King's Corridor) The Dining Room

The North Passage
Pictures
Includes:
Sir John Astley of Maidstone, Kent, Master of the Revels (i.e. Entertainments Manager) to King James I; he liked red trousers and had the best beard in the family.
Henry VIII; from the studio of Hans Holbein.
Rhoda Apreece, wife of Captain Francis Blake Delaval; together they completed Seaton Delaval Hall; and they were the parents of the 'Gay Delavals'; 1725, painted by John Vanderbank.

Furniture
Lacquer *cabinet*, Nagasaki, early 18th-century, on George III Chinese-style stand.

The Dining Room
(originally the Laundry)
Pictures
North (window) wall
Rhoda Delaval, wife of Sir Edward Astley, painted *c.*1755 by Arthur Pond, who also taught Rhoda painting.
Sir Jacob Henry Astley, son of Edward and Rhoda, who inherited Seaton Delaval in 1814 and commissioned John Dobson to make repairs to the house. Painted in 1805 by Benjamin Burnell.

Opposite Sir John Astley, Master of Revels to James I; painted c.1630

Below Rhoda Delaval; painted by Arthur Pond c.1755

West wall

Sir Jacob Astley, grandson of Rhoda and Edward Astley. He had owned Seaton Delaval for only five years when the great fire of 1822 destroyed the main block. He may have started repairs before his death in 1859. In 1841 the family's ancient title of Baron Hastings was recreated for him as 16th Lord Hastings. Painted in 1825 by Henry William Pickersgill.

East wall

Sir Jacob Astley, 16th Lord Hastings, hunting with fox hounds at Melton Constable. Painted before 1827 by Edwin Cooper.

South wall

Music Party, with Sir Jacob Astley, great-grandfather of the 16th Lord Hastings. Painted in 1732 by John Theodore Heins. *Windsor Castle*, painted by Hendrik Danckerts, c.1670. This painting was presented to the Astley family by King Charles II because of its loyalty in the Civil War.

Furniture

Includes: part of a set of walnut *dining chairs* with original red leather seats and curving legs carved with bunched feathers, the Astley family crest; of the time of King George I, c.1720; oval *wine cooler*, brass-bound mahogany with hinged top, c.1770; curving 'serpentine' *sideboard*, polished mahogany; c.1790; *dining table*, mahogany, c.1820; white-painted *sideboard and two side-tables*; in style of George III, but the sideboard made about a century later, c.1890, and the tables made later still to match.

Sculpture

Includes: two bronze groups of the *Marly Horses*, French, 19th-century.

The North-west Stair
The North Passage
The Bird Bedroom
The Drawing Room
The East Bedroom

The North-west Stair

Once a plain stone servants' stair, but refitted with timber treads and ornamental handrail.

Pictures

At the landing: *Portrait of the late Lady Hastings*, 1966, by Vasco Lazzolo.

The North Passage

Pictures

North side

The late Lord Hastings, 1970, by Vasco Lazzolo.
Henry Nevill, 3rd Marquess of Abergavenny, 1930, by Oswald Birley. He was the present Lord Hastings's great-grandfather.

South side

Sir Edward Astley, 4th Bt, husband of Rhoda Delaval, wearing Van Dyck costume; 1769, by Francis Cotes.
Blanche Astley and her younger brother, Edward; 1732, by John Theodore Heins.
Sir Francis Blake Delaval, KB (1727–71), *c*.1760, after Sir Joshua Reynolds; the owner of Seaton Delaval from 1752 until his death, 'Frank' was the stage-struck, spendthrift leader of the 'Gay Delavals' in their dramatic endeavours and partying. This painting was cut down after being damaged in the fire of 1822. It should show Sir Francis standing, full-length, holding a musket with

bayonet in his right hand, which has been cut off on the left side of the picture. Full-length versions of the portrait survive, notably one at Doddington, the family's former Lincolnshire house.

Ceramics
Display case includes Sèvres and Meissen. On top of case: three Meissen owls.

The Bird Bedroom
Originally a servant's bedroom which now has a decent range of mahogany furniture, and good view over the west (originally kitchen) yard to the gardens.

The Drawing Room
It was created by the late Lord and Lady Hastings from former servants' rooms in the 1980s. Located on the exposed north end of the house, the room was equipped with, and in winter certainly needed, a fireplace at each end.

Pictures
West wall
Rhoda Apreece, wife of Captain Francis Blake Delaval; painted *c*.1740 by Thomas Hudson.

South wall
Isabella Astley (1724–41), short-lived younger sister of Edward Astley, husband of Rhoda Delaval; painted in 1732 by John Theodore Heins Senior.
Labelled as the daughter of Charles I and Henrietta Maria, but apparently Lady Mary Villiers, daughter of the Duke of Buckingham; painted *c*.1635 in imitation of Van Dyck.
Anna Maria Astley, wearing a white dress and matching cap; daughter of Edward Astley, painted *c*.1768 by Francis Cotes.

Furniture
Includes: a giltwood *mirror*, *c*.1740; a curving 'serpentine' *chest of drawers*, rosewood; French

c.1740; pair of mahogany 'Gainsborough' *armchairs* with padded backs and elbow rests, *c*.1770; a tall English *cabinet* on stand in the Chinese style of Ince and Mayhew, *c*.1780; large Louis XIV-style boulle *table* with elaborate inlays and gilt bronze borders and decoration, *c*.1850; a pair of boulle *side-tables*, also mid-19th-century; a gilt-bronze *mantel clock* in Louis XV style, but late 19th-century, by Le Faucheur.; an inlaid mahogany 'cylinder' writing *bureau*; in Louis XVI style, but *c*.1890.

The East (or William Morris) Bedroom
Currently being used for conservation work visible through the internal windows from the Gallery: Items include the surcoat worn by Sir Jacob Astley at the Battle of Edgehill in 1642 – when he prayed: 'Lord, Thou knowest how busy I must be this day. If I forget Thee, do not Thou forget me.'

Below *Rhoda Apreece*; by Thomas Hudson, *c*.1740

The Gallery

Above **The Gallery**

Originally, this was a corridor giving access between two upstairs sections of servants' accommodation in the kitchen wing, which were divided by the two-storey kitchen. It may also have been used by the family for exercise when the weather was bad.

Pictures

Includes:

Full-length portraits of *Lord and Lady Delaval, and their son and four daughters*, painted in 1770s by William Bell.

Sarah Hussey, Mrs Robert Apreece. Mother of Rhoda Apreece and thus grandmother of John Lord Delaval and the other 'Gay Delavals'; *c*.1700.

Admiral Sir Ralph Delaval (knighted 1690; died 1707), an older cousin of Admiral George Delaval, for whom Seaton Delaval Hall was built; painted *c*.1695–1700, originally as a three-quarter-length portrait but enlarged to full length probably to form one of the family set in the 1770s.

Furniture

Includes: a pair of *black lacquer cabinets*, Japanese mid-17th-century, on early 19th-century English stands; a set of *walnut seats – two sofas and eight chairs* – of the time of Queen Anne *c*.1710; each with padded back and seat upholstered in needlework with pictures telling the story of Sir John Astley, King's Champion victorious in two mid-15th-century combats; a pair of gilt green *pier-tables* with grey veined marble tops elaborately carved with claw feet and central lions' masks hung with draperies simulating lions' skins and hanging claws; *c*.1740 (once stood in the Entrance Hall of the Central Block); pair of Anglo-Dutch *side-chairs* with deeply curved backs; *c*.1700–10.